Erma Bombeck

Erma Bombeck

Her funniest moments from

"At Wit's End"

Illustrated by Janet Cleland

Hallmark Editions

Selected by Barbara Loots.

Erma Bombeck

I have always said if the Good Lord had meant for me to speak in the mornings, He'd have put a recording in my chest and a string in the back of my neck.

Have a Good Day!

The mornings are bad for me. During the night everything has wrinkled: my skin, the clothes to be worn that day, the lunch meat. The dog (who has kidneys the size of barleycorn) is impatient to be let out.

The shoes that were left in the middle of the living room have moved on. The bread is frozen. While the kids shower, the mirror fogs up and my husband's beard goes limp. He's a bleeder.

I waste twenty minutes trying to make thirty-five cents out of two quarters and five pennies. My son mistakenly grabs the garbage (which he forgot to take out the night before) for his lunch and yells, "I'll eat it on the bus." My husband removes ice from the car with a pancake turner and scratches the windshield. He yells, "Have a good day!" and I yell back, "You have it! I had it yesterday."

Once every three years I have sauerkraut for dinner. Once every three years my husband has it for lunch. It always falls on the same day.

A REAL friend is fat when you are fat, depressed when you are depressed, and overdrawn when you are overdrawn.

Household Risks

No one appreciates how a woman must fight for her very life from hour to hour. The risks involved in preparing a meal alone are mind boggling. A year ago September, I was taking frozen Mexican TV dinners out of the freezer. One slipped out of my hand and I was nearly crippled by a frozen enchilada.

Who Says Money Can't Buy Happiness?

The other night my husband was squinting over a book when he said, "How big is the light bulb in this lamp?"

"I think it is 40 watts," I said.

"You have a bigger one in your sewing machine. How much would a 150-watt light bulb cost?"

"About 89 cents."

He recorded 89 cents on a slip of paper. "And how about salt and pepper shakers for the table? I've heard of some families that have one set for the stove and one for the table. How much would an extra set cost?"

"You could get a little cheapie for a buck or so."

He scribbled down $1 and continued, "What are pencils selling for these days? The little wooden ones that you put by the phone and write down messages when someone calls?"

"I think pencils are still a dime or 15 cents. What are you doing?"

"I see. And what about a simple comb? One that I could have for my very own without hair in it that doesn't match mine. Are they out of sight?"

"A comb costs about 29 cents."

"Very good. Now, what about a whole newspaper?"

"A what?"

"A whole newspaper. One that hasn't been turned inside out, clipped, folded, bent, spindled, mutilated and littered all over the bathroom before I get to read it?"

"Fifteen cents," I said tiredly.

"Incredible!" he said, touching a ball-point pen to his tongue. "Are they still selling those little woven cushions for the car seat? The ones that are new and don't have the metal springs ripping into your leg every time you slide into the seat?"

"Write down $3.98," I said.

"Oh, and what about those little tables that some people put their forks and tongs on when they cook out-of-doors instead of using a garbage can lid?"

"They would run you about $5.95."

Busily, he tallied up the total. "Can you believe it? $12.41 would not only buy me happiness, it would buy me ecstasy!"

That's the recession for you. There was a time when $12.41 would have bought hysteria!

I Told You I Was Sick

I could be suffering from a dinosaur bite and my doctor would say, "Everyone in town's got it. Just go to bed, take a lot of liquids, and call me if the leg falls off."

No one knows what their life expectancy is, but I have a horror of leaving this world and not having anyone in the entire family know how to replace a toilet tissue spindle.

Someday they will make one tombstone for housewives everywhere with a standard inscription. It will read, "I TOLD YOU I WAS SICK."

My Washer, My Monster

The plain and simple truth is washers were never meant to be domesticated.

I never see a Frankenstein movie but that I don't visualize a washer on a table in a laboratory ... with lights flashing, test tubes bubbling and slowly the washer begins to pulsate and the dial turns slowly to pre-soak, the lid begins to jiggle, and a monster is born.

A monster with a mind of its own who can fade things pink in an all white load, put lint on socks that are washed alone, and know the exact day when the warranty expires.

Day by day I see the washers of this country getting smarter and smarter. I saw one the other day that is programmed to pre-soak, release the bleach, add the soap, and cut loose the softener. The only thing it needs a human for is to tear the machine apart looking for the mates to all the socks.

That's Style!

If there is anything I admire in this world, it's people with "style."

Like the guy I read about last week who broke out of prison, secured a horse at the gate, and galloped down the road to freedom like a country gentleman.

That's "style."

Some of us go through life with the labels hanging out of our dresses, and our stomachs rumbling like a volcano during benediction. Our fresh chickens leak through the bottom of our grocery bags. Our curlers make creases in our faces that only surgery can erase, and on the first day we wear white shoes, we get an unseasonal snowfall.

Liberated as a Beaver

You're looking at a woman who hasn't been liberated very long—a week ago last Thursday to be exact.

Who knows why it took me so long to be converted, except I'm your average housewife who is a product of the 1950s. And as my liberated neighbor, Wanda, pointed out, those were insufferable times for women. We ate frozen waffles, bought store-bought Christmas cards, painted by numbers and covered our furniture with Con-Tac. Aprons were nothing more than a piece of concrete at the end of the driveway.

But as Wanda pointed out a week ago last Thursday, "You can't go on living your life vicariously through Sara Lee and Colonel Sanders. You're a person and a creative one at that. You have to create a role for yourself, one that you can be proud of. Aren't you tired of being a sex object?"

(Would you excuse me a moment? I think my ceramic Madonna is burning in the kiln.)

Where was I? Oh yes, creating a role for myself. Wanda said I'd have to get into knitting needles and needlepoint as a way of expression. Personally, I have always felt if the Good Lord had meant for needles to be invented, he would never have given us bare feet, but it did prove to be an extension of me I had never known. I crocheted three chignon caps, and when my hair grows out I'll have the warmest chignon in town.

(Hang on, I think my homemade yogurt is ready to take out of the warmer.)

Wanda was the first to help me grind flour in preparation for my first loaf of home-baked bread. It not only broadened my world, but you wouldn't believe what it did for my hips.

(Oh, good grief. You know what I smelled? It wasn't the Madonna in the kiln, it was the wax for the batik wall hanging I'm making. I guess it's like tie-dye — you ruin a lot of stuff before you become fulfilled.)

Wanda called yesterday just as I was pouring the candle wax into a milk carton. "Just checking on you," she laughed. "According to our time schedule, you have a job interview for this afternoon, a course in car mechanics this evening, you picket a beauty pageant tomorrow morning and strip the paint off your dresser and start your organic gardening tomorrow afternoon."

I'm glad Wanda called. Sometimes I get very morose remembering how I used to be when I was a pampered, indulged sex object.

Why I Stopped Talking to Plants

I can tell you the exact day I stopped talking to my indoor plants.

I was sitting alone at the bedside of a failing houseplant and sympathizing, "Poor baby. You can tell me. Your tail is dragging because you are pot bound, isn't it?"

From the kitchen, the voice of the milkman shouted, "No, Ma'am, I just have a little head cold."

At that moment I saw myself for what I really was...a converted plant molester trying to make up for all my past sins. But it was too late for a woman who tore the leaves off a philodendron for a bookmark, who let her fern die of terminal dust and who planted a coffee bean tree in Play-Doh to pick up the color scheme of the hallway.

It just wasn't natural for a full-grown woman to sit around humming to her plants. So from that day on, I never talked to the plants again. Now I just sit around like a normal person, talking and laughing to myself.

For years I have been made to feel less than maternal because I feel less than adequate in the kitchen. (As my husband says, "Get out of there before you kill someone.")

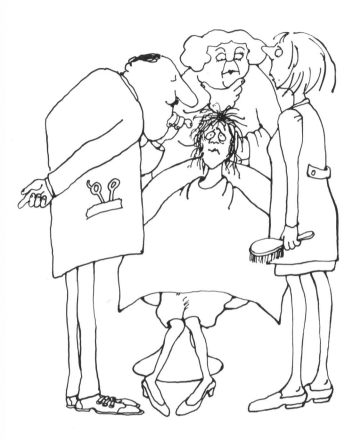

Probably my finest hour came last week when one son dropped me off at the beauty shop with instructions to "Call when they're finished with the estimate."

How I Find Things

I have just figured out that I have spent a total of twenty-three years, four months, six days, twelve hours and seventeen minutes looking for things around the house that are not really lost. (If I had spent that much time taking care of my face and body, I could be a love goddess by now.)

The other morning as I hung by my heels retrieving the innards of the coffeepot from the garbage can, my husband, in one of his rare moments of sentiment, said, "You have the instincts of a water buffalo. You eventually find everything. I don't know how you do it."

This is my formula for finding things around the house before they get lost. Here is how it works. First, you must ask yourself, "If I were an iced tea spoon who wanted to get away for a few days, where would I hide?" Then you call on experience. Small boys hate to take medicine. Right? They often drink their orange juice from an old-fashioned glass just to be different. Thus, they have probably taken their cold syrup from an iced tea spoon. The iced tea spoon then is in the medicine chest.

Now, let's see, if I were an envelope and a stamp who hated crowds, where would I go?

Clever and Creative

Twenty-two years ago, as a bride, I went through my Clever and Creative syndrome. I drove a four-inch spike into my kitchen wall over the sink and speared my unpaid bills on it. When a neighbor looked at it and remarked, "That looks like a four-inch spike with a bunch of unpaid bills on it," I became incensed and never again was clever and creative.

I was reading an article the other day on creativity and realized the most creative thing our family did together was to discover our *TV Guide* had expired.

Your Close-Knit Family, We're Not

We have never been what you might call your close-knit family...even at the dinner table. The last time someone had his arm around another, our son had a chicken bone caught in his throat. My daughter grabbed him, horror written on her face, and she screamed hysterically, "For the love of heaven! Someone help him! He's choking to death and it's his turn for dishes!"

"The trouble with your tennis," said my husband, sliding on his sweatband, "is that you talk too much. The name of the game is concentration."

"You know, I think you're right," I said, revving up for a serve. "Incidentally, the garage called and your transmission is gone."

He stood there numb as the ball bounced off his foot.

"THE TRANSMISSION!"

"That's fifteen-love. Yep, it couldn't come at a worse time. We got an estimate on Brucie's mouth today and the tab comes to $1500. In two years I figure our orthodontist will buy Iran. Ready?"

He swiped pathetically at the next serve and missed it.

"That's thirty-love. Let's not talk about depressing things. Let's just play tennis. By the way, what does the IRS want with you?"

He dropped the racket as I served the next ball.

"I have no idea. Did they call?"

"Forty-love. I put the message on the refrigerator."

"Hold it!" he said coming to the net. "Do you mean to tell me the IRS called and you didn't tell me the moment I walked in the door?"

"I didn't want to upset you during dinner. If I did, I would have told you my mother is coming

16

for a visit, we are overdrawn at the bank, your watch fell in the disposal, there's a story in tonight's paper about the cutback at your firm, and your son ran away from home. But enough small talk."

He massaged his head with his hand as he dragged into position for my next serve.

"Dear," I smiled, "you are in the wrong court. Do you mind moving over to where I expect to serve?"

"What?" he asked, his eyes staring vacantly.

"Move over. There. If I make this point I want to talk with you about the divorce."

"Divorce?" he winced, stumbling over his shoelace.

"My game!" I said. "Yes, Bernice and Brute, the couple we met in Canada about six years ago. Remember them?"

"You know what you are?" he stormed. "You are unreal. I have never seen a woman so intent on destroying a man's game. Is there anything else before I..."

"Look," I interrupted. "Are we going to stand here and talk all day or are we going to play some serious tennis?"

The Terrible Twos

I have written two books, play a ukelele and can drive a car without looking at my feet, but do you know what singular thing impresses women when I am in a group? The fact that I have survived a two-year-old.

In all modesty, I must admit I am not the only woman in North America to endure the terrible twos, but I am possibly one of the few who can talk about it without knotting my handkerchief.

One of the reasons I think I was so successful is that I adjusted earlier than most women. My kids were born being two years old. They seemed to have a full set of teeth for biting, an emergency supply of saliva for spitting and little legs that ran the mile under three minutes.

One evening I said to my husband, "I cannot go on like this. I am exhausted."

He said, "You're just a little tired."

"When you fall asleep on an obscene phone call," I said, "you're exhausted."

"Do you mean to tell me a bald baby a yard high with a smile that could defrost Mount Everest is getting you down?"

"You don't understand," I said. "Between 8:30 A.M. and 12:30 P.M., he put the cat in the dryer, got his arm caught in a rake, put his training pants in the oven, ate a guppy, pulled over the flour canister, sat on my geraniums, put his

18

orthopedic shoes in the bathtub, dropped a television knob down the register, tore up my card for jury duty and talked fifteen minutes without operator assistance to a housewife in New Mexico."

"Have you tried naps?" asked my husband.

"I've tried, but he keeps crawling in my playpen and slobbering, 'Mama, play...'"

Who's Who of What??

No one was more surprised than I to receive a questionnaire from England wanting to include me in Vol. II of the International Who's Who in Community Service.

This is quite an honor for a woman who (a) got pregnant so she wouldn't have to go on a field trip to a canning factory with the third grade; (b) sent out cards to 200 sports booster parents inviting them to be "athletic supporters"; and (c) was relieved of my duties as PTA hospitality chairman when I served watercress salad with my house dressing — gin and tonic.

A Gardener Has No Friends

This year, there are sixty million Americans who are planting vegetable gardens.

Have you any idea what it means to have sixty million tillers of the soil running loose?

I'll give it to you straight. It means there will have to be at least 210 million tillees to eat the stuff at harvest time, and frankly, I don't think we have the population to handle it.

At last count, there were eighty million adult non-gardeners in this country. Of this amount, thirty-two million are allergic to tomatoes and their faces break out after eating the first bushel. Twenty-eight million are still eating bread-and-butter pickles they canned in 1958, and of the remaining twenty million, eighteen million had their teeth turn green during July and August.

To begin with, the harvest of a home garden never occurs when the gardener is at home. He is always on vacation. I don't know how this phenomenon occurs, but I have known tillers who have hung around all summer waiting for their labors to bear fruit. They leave a few hours for a dental appointment only to return and realize they've missed the harvest.

Another phenomenon is that you can share your garden with friends. After the first five hundred pounds of bib lettuce, a gardener has no friends.

I know the work involved in gardening and it is gratifying that the American people are intent on solving the food problem, but the real heroes of the war against inflation have to be the non-gardeners who smile and burp, "Why, everyone can use another bushel of radishes!"

Do you know what the odds are against polishing off every opened box of breakfast cereal in your cupboard?

Well, we've done it. The hard way. With kids.

For the last fifteen years we have had no less than a dozen or so half-eaten boxes of Fortified Blinkies, Cackly Krunchies, Captain Sugar, Dry Ryes, Toasted Wrigglies, Heap of Honey and Cavity Krispies. Regardless of what you have been told, these cereals didn't snap, crackle, or pop. They just laid there on the shelves year after year and turned stale.

About a month ago I made an announcement at breakfast. "There will be no more cereal purchased in this house until we eat up every single box that is opened."

They were shocked momentarily. Then, "Why?"

"Because I can no longer afford to support twelve boxes of opened cereal. Take this box of Bloated Oats (I wish someone would). Originally, I bought it for thirty-nine cents. As you will remember, it contained a full-size nuclear submarine, complete with a crew of 120, and secret plans for occupying Connecticut. As you may also remember, I inadvertently ate the sub causing a chipped tooth that cost me $85.

"When the cereal didn't move at our breakfast

table, I ran out into the snow one morning in my bedroom slippers to hustle it to some starving birds who pecked once at it then migrated forever. The antibiotics for my cold cost me $13.

"This cereal has also been with us through three moves which, counting the packing, shipping, and crating, cost around $15.42. It also attracted ants in the new house which put me back $2.72 for traps. All tolled, this crummy box of cereal has cost us $116.53. Eat up!"

This morning we went to the grocery store. At the cereal shelves, they scattered. "Hold it!" I said. "We are all going to agree on one box of cereal." What ensued may set retailing back thirty years.

"I hate Bran Brittles. They're for old people with irregularities."

"And I hate Chock Full of Soggies that turn your teeth purple."

"Let's get Jungle Jollies. They don't have any nutrition whatsoever."

Miraculously, they appeared with a single box. "We've all decided on Mangled Wheat Bits."

"That's great," I said. "Any particular reason?"

"Yeah, there's a magic kit inside guaranteed to make anything disappear."

Things My Mother Taught Me

One of my kids had an English assignment the other night to do a paper on "Things My Mother Taught Me."

I couldn't help but be flattered as he wrote feverishly in his notebook for the better part of forty-five minutes. When he was finished, I asked, "Do you mind if I read it?"

He shrugged, "Okay. If you want to, but don't get it dirty."

THINGS MY MOTHER TAUGHT ME

Logic: "If you fall off that swing and break your neck, you are not going to the store with me."

Medicine: "If you don't stop crossing your eyes, they are going to freeze that way!" (There is no cure, no telethon and no relief for frozen eyes.)

Optimism: "You are going to enjoy yourself at that birthday party or I am going to break every bone in your body."

Philosophy: "You show me a boy with a pet snake and I'll show you a boy who wants his mother dead!"

ESP: "Put on the sweater! Don't you think I know when you are cold?"

Science: "You put your hand out of the car window and it'll blow off." (Gravity: What goes out, must blow off.)

Insight: "Do you realize that fifty million children in southeast Asia consider broccoli a treat...like ice cream?" (How do you get a broccoli deficiency?)

Finance: "I told you the tooth fairy is writing checks because computerized billing is easier for the IRS."

Challenge: "Where is your sister and don't talk with food in your mouth. Answer me!"

Ethics: "If are too busy to take out the garbage, you are too busy to need an allowance."

Genealogy: "Shut that door. Or were you born in a barn?" (You're asking me?)

Suspense: "Can you guess what I found under your bed today?"

Humor: "When that lawn mower cuts off your toes, don't come running to me."

I took off my glasses and put down the paper. Son of a gun. I would have been willing to bet during all those years he hadn't heard a word I said.

Diets Are Getting on My Nerves

I'm sick to death of pouring one-calorie soft drinks over my ice cream, using imitation mayonnaise in my potato salad, and ruining a perfectly good gravy sandwich by pouring it between two slices of diet bread.

I come from a home where gravy is a beverage.

I have dieted continuously for the last two decades and lost a total of 758 pounds. By all calculations, I should be hanging from a charm bracelet.

I walked by a hall mirror the other day and sucked in my stomach. NOTHING MOVED!

Super Children

I often find myself at the mercy of women with Super Children. Super Children are unmitigated joy. They can always be counted on to do and say the right thing. They always make the team, have fewer cavities, skip acne, know what they want to be in the third grade, have their paper displayed at Open House, and always remember to bring home the Mother's Day card from art class.

I have made a study of Super Children and

have come to the conclusion that the only difference between Super Children and Normal Kids is in the interpretation. For example:

NORMAL KIDS	SUPER CHILDREN
Forgetful	Preoccupied
Fat	Healthy
Sloppy beasts	Academically geared
Weirdo who won't get a haircut	Nonconformist
Lazy bum	Deep thinker
Flunked out	Victim of a poor teacher
TV addict	TV critic
Cut from the team	Saved from a prejudiced coach
Forgot me on Mother's Day	Is saving his money for my operation
Oversleeps in the morning	A recessive gene

At one time I was so naive I thought only edible things belonged in the refrigerator, bicycles without wheels should be discarded and if you had eight people to dinner, all the glasses had to match.

27

I Think I'm Getting Older

No one, unless they've been there, can appreciate the physical and emotional traumas of reaching forty. Your body reacts like a steam iron on the last day of warranty. It dies on you.

Getting old is discovering your priest smells like bubble gum, your lawyer is fighting acne, and your son's math teacher is wearing a training bra.

Everyone knows middle age is ten years from wherever you are.

The Leftover

One morning I opened my refrigerator door and immediately slammed it shut as my whole body turned into a block of fear.

"What's the matter?" asked my husband.

"Don't open this door! There's a blob in there!"

"There's always a blob in there," he said dryly. "Let me see if I can identify the year on this one."

"You open that door and we're finished. I tell you it's like the one I saw last night on the late movie."

He coaxed me aside and opened the door. "You're right," he said. "With a little nudge, this leftover could annihilate New Jersey."

Last week I gave a luncheon for eight women who are all on different diets. It was like hosting a famine.

The Art of Unwinding

Everyone I knew was into some kind of stitchery, and one day as my friend, Terri, sat needle-pointing a calendar, I said, "How do you have the patience?"

"Patience," she laughed. "This is the most re-laxing thing I do all day. You're tense. You should get yourself something to unwind."

That's when I bought Country Gardens, a stamped piece of linen in a kit with twenty-eight colors of yarn and instructions for eighteen stitches.

Ever since, Country Gardens has never left my side. It is like an appendage growing out of my fingers. I started it one morning when the kids left for school. At three when they wandered home, I was still at it and continued on through the night.

Unwinding was a full-time job. The children bugged me constantly, demanding food, answers to questions, and first aid when they bled. The other morning as I stitched feverishly one of them came up to my elbow and said, "Mom." I jumped a foot off the chair. "Can't you see I'm relaxing?" I said. "I don't suppose you've ever heard of appointments. If you want me to make time for you I can, but don't just 'drop in.' Be-sides, why aren't you at school?"

"It's Saturday," he said simply.

My husband says I am possessed. The other morning about two A.M., he leaned over and said, "You have relaxed enough," and flipped off the light. I don't know what kind of an animal would turn off your light in the middle of a French knot. I cried myself to sleep.

Yesterday Terri dropped in (without an appointment) and suggested I relax more. "You are pale, your eyes are red from strain, and frankly I get more fun out of burping my Tupperware than talking to you anymore."

I figure if I can work straight through, without interruption, Country Gardens should be finished and framed by the first week of November. Then I may take a few days off and be tense.

After all, all play and no work can kill you.

Child Psychology

Just about the time I had my first child, all the psychologists were coming out with their new theories on discipline. One day as I prepared to give my daughter a thump on the rump, a neighbor warned, "Do you want to permanently damage her id?"

Damage it! I didn't even know where it was.

Are We Rich?

Being rich is a relative sort of thing. Here's how I can always tell:

You're rich when you buy your gas at the same service station all the time so your glasses match.

You're rich when you can have eight people to dinner and don't have to wash forks between the main course and dessert.

You're rich when you buy clothes for your kids that are two sizes too big for the one you buy 'em for and four sizes too big for the one that comes after him.

You're rich when you own a boat...without oars.

You know people are loaded when they don't have to save rubber bands from the celery and store them on a doorknob.

You're rich when your dog is wet and smells good.

You're rich when your own hair looks so great everyone thinks it's a wig.

A leading appliance manufacturer has just come out with a refrigerator that can play music, record recipes, teach you a foreign language or talk back to your kids.

If it could cry, it could be a mother.

The Telephone Crisis

In talking with a working mother the other day, she disclosed one of the little-discussed hazards of holding down a job with one hand and tending a family with the other. She called it the "Telephone Crisis."

At least once a day, a working mother will be summoned to the business phone to hear the voice of her child say, "Mom, can I make a raft and mess around on the Ohio River with Huckleberry Hickey?"

"If you want to find out how indispensable you really are," said one mother, "just get a job and wait for the phone to ring. My kids have had me called out of conferences involving thousands of dollars to electrify me with such breathless decisions as:

1. Can I split a Pepsi with Kathy?
2. Guess what the dog dug up?
3. Did you wash my white shorts for gym tomorrow?
4. I got an 83 on my health test.
5. Rick just got his driver's license. Can I go with him to town and see how he does in traffic?"

Hire a Husband

For years I have held down two jobs while my husband sat back and watched like it was a replay of the Dust Bowl.

That is about to change. The International Labor Organization has called on husbands to shoulder a bigger share of the household chores as one way to ease the burden carried by married women who work.

"I think they are absolutely right," said my husband. "Women are overworked trying to balance two jobs. Huffing and puffing, eyes on the clock, picking up kids, ironing at night, shopping for food on their day off. Why don't you try and find some husband to come in and help a couple days a week."

"You don't understand, Jr.," I said. "They're talking about you!"

"I don't do floors or windows," he said quickly.

"That's no problem. I assume you drive."

"Yes, but I bowl on Tuesdays, watch eighty-six hours of sports a week on TV and sleep in."

"We can work something out."

"I'm not finished yet. I don't mend, scrub, scour, bake, plumb, or dunk diapers up and down in the johns. I don't defrost, wax, move furniture, paint woodwork or take empties back to the store."

"Are you finished?"

"I haven't even started. I don't cut bubble gum out of hair, pack lunches, pick up cleaning, fix the electric garage door, fertilize the grass, iron, compress garbage, wash the dog, do dishes, replace toilet tissue spindles, or clean up after a sick child at three in the morning.

"I don't take telephone messages, mend broken shoestrings, kiss a bloody knee, dust, water plants, work weekends, holidays and on my birthday, or fiddle with checks."

"That's perfectly all right," I smiled. "You can start by picking up the boys' bedroom."

An hour and a half later, I pushed open the door. "How are you making out?"

"Terrific!" he said. "I've read fifteen comic books, put together eight miles of track for my car...it's the little red one...found my flashlight under the bed I've been looking for for two years, and haven't had anyone bug me for an hour and a half. You know, I don't know what you women have to complain about."

My husband believes if God had meant for man to put a nail in the wall, He would have given him a rubber thumb.

One hates to be dramatic, but sever my phone cord and I bleed to death.

How come pens never have any ink in them except when you forget and put them in the washer and your entire laundry turns blue?

If the national average of children is 2.3, how come every car off the assembly line only has two back windows?

How come the wheels on my shopping cart won't turn in the supermarket, but when I start to empty the groceries from it into the car, it oils in and out of traffic in front of cars and people as if it had a motor attached to it?

How did my crock pot know the exact day the warranty ran out?

Why do four out of every five Americans insist on eating in their own car when everything in the car slants?

Why do I tell everyone that I'm raising my children to think for themselves... and feel crummy when they do?

I love reading household hints on how to cut your food budget, but then I've always loved fiction.

The Sleek Generation

I've seen it coming for some time. With every generation the women seem to get healthier and healthier. (I have a friend so healthy she has to lean against a wall for balance.)

Researchers say we have brought it on ourselves. We take too good care of our children, plying them with vitamins, balancing their diets, providing them with recreational facilities. I defy you to line up the last two generations and compare. Beside my daughter I look like a quail.

She is definitely a station wagon model... built long, sleek and always consuming something. I am small, compact and impossible to get into gear.

When You Can Afford It . . .

It's the old saw—when you need it, you can't afford it...when you can afford it, you can't enjoy it.

We used to drive around on Sundays and look at houses built to accommodate a growing family. The only ones who could afford them were couples whose children had grown.

It's cruel to even bring it up, but here are just a few of the observations that are probably in your future and mine.

When your husband can afford to have his hair styled, he may have nothing left to rearrange.

When you can afford to have your hair frosted, your teen-agers may have streaked it for you.

When you can afford sexy clothes, you'll have forgotten why you are wearing them.

When you can afford to "get away from it all," it will take more effort to go than to stay.

When someone gets around to baking you a birthday cake, the candles will be a fire hazard.

Some Fears Are Normal

I have always had a theory that some fears are normal...that it is abnormal to be able to keep breathing when you see a flashing red police car light in your rearview mirror...to remain conscious when the oxygen mask drops down before you on an airplane...to keep cool when you hear your doctor whisper to your nurse, "ARE YOU SURE?"...to remain calm when you are called by the principal in the middle of the afternoon who says, "Your son has something he wants to tell you."

A Dog's Life

I kept a diary of our first seven days with our puppy, Bow Wow.

Day I: Bow Wow has been in the house fourteen hours, during which time his feet have never touched the floor.

He has been fed eight times, burped five, danced on the TV set, slid down the banister, been given a bath, blown dry with my hair dryer, visited twelve homes, ridden a bicycle and barked long distance on the telephone. At the moment, he is asleep under a dual-control thermal blanket.

Day II: Bow Wow continues to reign. It took eight saucepans to warm his dinner. Tonight the children put on a puppet show for Bow Wow. He watched it from a pillow that I had just needle-pointed at a cost of $12. Bow Wow got to stand on the floor tonight and headed for the door. One child shoved the other into the hall tree. The other one slapped his brother, while the third one lurched for the dog and opened the door first.

Day III: At three this morning, one of the children complained that Bow Wow was keeping them awake with his howling. When I suggested he be fed, he said his brother did it, who vowed his sister did it, who said, "It's not my turn." Bow Wow chewed up my evening slipper and put everyone into stitches.

Day IV: Bow Wow blew Show and Tell. He showed too much and didn't have a finish. A clean-up committee of one was delegated to do the honors. One of the children said if the dog followed him to school one more time and he had to bring him home he was going to kick him. I suspect the newness is wearing off.

Day V: There was a rule made on Day I that the first one to spot a puddle automatically cleaned it up. The entire household is suffering from indoor blindness. Today, Bow Wow chewed up a catcher's mitt. No one was amused.

Day VI: Today, I yelled, "Has anyone seen Bow Wow?"

Day VII: One of the kids yelled back, "Who?"

I tried to find six women who could transport Miss Bilk's second grade on a field trip to the phone company. It made the invasion of Normandy look like an impulse.

The New Morality

The other day I passed the bedroom of one of my teen-agers. The music was deafening as a mob of kids sat around the floor swilling soft drinks and grinding potato chips into the carpet.

"Aren't you apprehensive about kids gathering around a bed?" asked a concerned friend.

"Are you crazy?" I said. "They'll never find it in that mess!"

Housework? What Housework?

Nothing has stirred me more than a quotation attributed to the late Eleanor Roosevelt. When she was asked if housekeeping bothered her she replied, "I rarely devote more than fifteen minutes a day to it."

Good Lord, that's beautiful.

I personally find fifteen minutes a day doing housework excessive, but it's the idea that counts.

When I was first married I broke my bones cleaning that apartment. Then one day, I was interrupted. "Where are you going?" asked my husband.

"I'm going to have a baby. I'll only be a minute or two."

That was twenty-two years ago and I never got back to housework as a formal religion.

I'm Worried About the Children...

The creative writing teacher said the most creative thing about our son was his spelling.

My kids never had the imagination or inclination to run away from home despite the fact I used to pack road maps in their lunches.

Like most mothers, I have a horror of my daughter getting married, inviting me to dinner and serving her specialty: a bowl of undercooked popcorn.

Frankly, I have always felt if God had meant for children to run the country, He would have made the seats in Congress out of plastic with a hole in the middle.

I would like to meet face to face the man who designed the child-proof cap. (Any fool knows Americans do not need a child-proof cap. If you have something you don't want within the reach of children, you just put it in a garbage bag, set it on the counter and yell, "Someone empty this!")

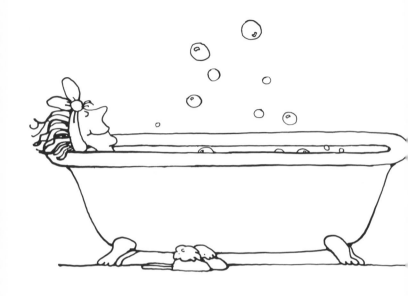

I'll Know When I've Made It

How does a wife and mother know it when she becomes a Superstar—a person in her own right?

I'll know.

One day the phone will ring and it will be for me.

I'll see my child in public, speak to him, and he'll recognize me.

One of these mornings, out of four cars in the

driveway one of them will be running and I'll get it.

Or the kids will set the table and someone else will get the bent fork.

I'll go out to dinner and no one will lean over and whisper just before the bill, "You cashed a check today, didn't you?"

Or I'll go through an entire evening without someone asking me for a nose tissue.

I'll cash a check at the supermarket and not have to leave a blood specimen.

I'll go through the express line with seven items.

I'll know I've become something special when someone turns to me before flipping the TV dial and asks, "Are you watching this?"

When I can have new medicine for my cold instead of using up what's left in the medicine chest.

When I can ask for a "doggy bag" and some smart aleck doesn't say, "You want to eat it here or to go?"

I don't know when, but one of these days it will happen — the respect I so richly deserve will be heaped upon me.

The other night my husband came in, looked around and said, "Isn't there anyone home?"

"I'm here," I said.

"C'mon. You know what I mean."

I knew.

Set in Janson, a distinguished Old Style face designed by Nicholas Kis and originally issued by Anton Janson in the late seventeenth century. Printed on Hallmark Eggshell Book paper. Designed by William Hunt.